Copyright

No part of this publication
transmitted in any form or b',
mechanical, photographing, recording, or any other means
of reproduction in use, without the prior written permission
of the author. Distribution of this e-book without the prior
written permission of the author is illegal, and therefore,
punishable by law.

Legal notice: The author and publisher of this book (and
any accompanying materials) have made their best efforts
in preparing the material. The author and publisher make
no representation or warranties with respect to the
accuracy, applicability, fitness, or completeness of the
contents of this book. The information contained in this
book is strictly for educational purposes. Therefore, if you
wish to apply ideas contained in this book, you are taking
full responsibility for your actions.

1

Be sure to check out Mike Riley's other books:

Murders Unsolved: Cases That Have Baffled The Authorities For Years

"The body was wrapped in a plaid blanket, and placed inside a box that had once held a baby's bassinet purchased from J.C. Penney's. The boy was clean and dry, and recently groomed. However, he looked to be undernourished. Clumps of hair found on the body suggested he had been groomed after death."

Check it out.

America's Early Serial Killers: Five Cases of Frontier Madness

"We tend to think of those early settlers as hard working, decent people only looking for religious freedom and better opportunities for their families. However, even during those times, people existed who were depraved, evil and mentally ill. These are some of their stories."

Check it out.

Table of Contents

Introduction

It is most people's greatest fear to lose a loved one too soon. When circumstance or the actions of others cause the loss, it is even more difficult to reconcile. However, when the lost one is never found, there is no closure, no way for those left behind to ever really get on with their lives

The following stories cover some of these mysteries from across the world, going back to the 16th century. They have left people wondering and questioning what happened. Still today these stories raise our curiosity and hold us spell bound, wondering what actually happened.

The possibility of recent scientific advances allowing some of these cases to actually be solved keep our interest alive and create great stories of intrigue to many people around the world.

Please enjoy the following stories.

An Early American Mystery: The Colonists of Roanoke Island

Missing Persons: The Missing Colonists of Roanoke Island
Date: 1590
Last Known Location: Roanoke Island, North Carolina

Backstory:
On May 8th, 1587, a group of men, women and children left England for a new life. They were excited by stories of the New World, and were headed to establish their own life there.

They were some of the first colonists of what is now know as Roanoke Island. In the late 16th century, attempts were made to establish a permanent English settlement in what is now Dare County, North Carolina. Sir Humphrey Gilbert, a half brother of Sir Walter Raleigh, originally organized the venture and provided the financial backing. After he had drowned in 1583 during another, aborted, attempt to colonize Newfoundland, his now famous half brother was able to gain the charter from the Queen and continue.

In an attempt to discover riches in the new world, and also create a base to launch ships on raids against treasure fleets of Spain, Queen Elizabeth I granted Raleigh the rights to establish a colony in North America on March 25th, 1584. By April 27th, Raleigh had organized a first expedition to North America, to explore along the east coast.

The expedition was lead by Philip Amadas and Arthur Barlowe, and landed at Roanoke Island on July 4th. The first expedition returned to England, reporting that they had established relationships with the native population named the Secotans and the Croatoans, and brought two of them back with them to describe the area to Raleigh. Based on these results, he then organized a second expedition, led by Sir Richard Grenville. It departed from Plymouth on April 9th, 1585.

Grenville's fleet consisted of five main ships. His own, named the Tiger, was separated from the others off the coast of Portugal, in an extreme storm. Following the pre-arranged contingency plan, he continued on to Puerto Rico, where he was supposed to meet up with the other ships. He arrived on May 11th, and while waiting, he built a fort and struck up relations with the Spanish natives. By June 7th no other ships had arrived, and so he decided to strike out on his own again. Despite ruining most of their food supplies when they struck a shoal, they managed to catch up to two other ships from the fleet in the Outer Banks.

An incident occurred soon after where natives were blamed for stealing a silver cup, and the settlers retaliated and burned their village. Despite this, and an ongoing issue surrounding a lack of food, Grenville left one hundred and seven men to establish the Roanoke Island colony. He promised to return in April 1586 with supplies.

By July 1586, there was no sign of his return, and relations with the natives were stressed and the settlers were now under attack themselves. Soon after this, Sir Francis Drake, an English sea captain, was passing by and offered to take the settlers back to England. They accepted and left, only to have Grenville return soon after to find the colony abandoned. Grenville returned to England, but left a small group behind to keep Raleigh's claim on the island.

In 1587, he sent a last group once more to officially establish a colony at Chesapeake Bay. John White, a friend of Raleigh's was among them. Raleigh later ordered White to travel to Roanoke and collect the remaining men. However, when they arrived they found no one, except a single unidentified skeleton. Rather than allowing the colonists to return to the ships, the commander Simon

Fernandez, instead insisted that they stay at Roanoke to establish a new colony.

Relations were tenuous with the natives due to previous encounters, and after a short time a colonist named Howe was alone searching for crabs, and was killed by a native. Now in fear for their lives, the colonists were this time able to persuade White to allow them to return to England to explain their situation and ask for help to protect the settlement. Around one hundred and fifteen were again left behind.

On The Day In Question:
For a number of reasons, including the weather and the Anglo-Spanish War, it was a number of years again before anyone was able to return to the settlement at Roanoke. An attempt in 1588 by White resulted in capture by Spanish ships and their cargo seized. With nothing to deliver, they turned back for England without ever visiting the colonists they had left behind.

It was another three years again before another attempt. White was able to join a private expedition that agreed to stop off at Roanoke. When he arrived, the settlement was deserted and there was not a single trace of any of the settlers, nor a single sign of battle.

There were but two clues left behind. The word *Croatoan* carved into a post of a fence and *Cro* carved into a tree.

Investigation:
At the time, relations with the native tribes were tenuous. Not all tribes were hostile, but some certainly were. Relationships between the two were already soured by attempts from the first colonists (who had later returned to England) to explore the area.

Perhaps one or more of the local native tribes decided to be done with the English once and for all? Was the engraving of the word *Croatoan* on the post pointing to the attackers?

Others hypothesize that after supplies or help failed to arrive for years, the settlers attempted to sail back to England themselves, and ran afoul of the Spaniards. Knowing of Raleigh's plans to use it as a base to attack their own ships, perhaps the Spanish ships decided to act first and destroy it. However, there is no hard evidence to support this.

In 1607, efforts were taken by settlers at the Jamestown colony to find out information as to what happened to the lost colonists. Captain John Smith, the then leader of the colony was the first to report definitive information. As reported by chronicler Samuel Purchas, Wahunsunacock (known in English as Chief Powhatan) had told Captain Smith that he had personally killed the colonists.

When the Chief's involvement was confirmed later by William Strachey, the then secretary of the colony, in a report, it was seen to confirm Smith's report as truth. The story persisted for more than four hundred years, however recent re-examination suggests that although there were slaughters conducted by the native tribe, none were of the Roanoke colony.

Current Status:
In 2012, a map drawn by White was re-discovered, having been forgotten for centuries. It revealed the planned location for the settlement, and also showed a fort where the settlers may have headed. The detail on the map was unclear from patches that had since been placed on the map and needed to be enhanced. However, these findings correlated to evidence from historian James Horn, who reports in his book that the settlers had discussed moving around fifty miles inland before White left them.

The team researching the map concluded that the most likely chance for survival was for the colonists to split up and disperse separately, which would make tracking them as a group in modern times incredibly difficult.

Today there is speculation that smaller groups of settlers may have travelled in different directions and were taken in by sympathetic tribes or villages. There were simply too many of them to be supported by any other groups as a whole.

Other evidence found also supports this theory. A map named the *Zuniga Map* drawn around 1607 states that 'four men clothed that came from roonock' joined a local Iroquois tribe and taught the tribe to build two story stone houses. At various times, European captives were sighted at various Indian settlements.

Throughout the 17th and 18th centuries, various reports of gray-eyed natives who claimed to be descended from the colonists emerged, along with reports of blond, blue-eyed natives from the Tuscaroras tribe. In the late 1880's, a state legislator from North Carolina named Hamilton McMillan noted that some of his Indian neighbors claimed to be descendants of the colonists.

He noticed that many words in their own language were very similar to obsolete English words from the time, and family names matched those from the colony's manifest. Similar claims also exist from other tribes, although no documented evidence of them exists.

Ground penetrating radar has also been used to identify a site that has some evidence that perhaps it was originally a settlement. However nothing conclusive to suggest the definitive location of the original Roanoke settlement, nor what happened to the colonists, has ever been found. Other archaeological investigations have also discovered some evidence to suggest habitation of Roanoke, but nothing concrete.

In 2005, the *Lost Colony DNA Project* was launched. The project is using DNA evidence to try to determine whether members of the colony integrated into local native tribes.

Despite all modern efforts however, to this day, the mystery of what happened to the settlers of Roanoke Island remains unsolved.

The Missing Author of *12 Years a Slave*: Solomon Northup

Missing Person: Solomon Northup
Date: 1863 (precise date unknown)
Last Known Location: Warren County, New York

Backstory:
Having recently been made into a feature film *12 Years a Slave*, the life story of Solomon Northup contains another intriguing mystery.

Northup was a free born African American, his father being a freed slave and his mother also a free woman of color. He owned land in New York and was a farmer and violinist. Northup's father was given his freedom in the will of his owner, Mr. Northup, prior to Solomon's birth.

Northup grew up in relatively good conditions for blacks at the time, and was an accomplished violin player. He married Anne Hampton on Christmas Day, 1829 and they had three children together, named Elizabeth, Margaret, and Alonzo. Northup was first a farmer like his father, but then sold the farm and moved to Saratoga Springs, New York. Here, he worked different jobs, including as a musician.

On The Day In Question:
In 1841, Northup (then thirty-two years old) had a meeting with two men, who introduced themselves as entertainers named Merrill Brown and Abram Hamilton. They offered him a job as a fiddler for a circus in New York City. Once they were in New York, the men were then able to convince Northup to continue on with them to perform with the circus in Washington D.C. He was offered a generous wage, as well as covering the costs of his return trip, making the offer no doubt very appealing.

Northup made sure to get a copy of his papers documenting his status as a free man, as he was traveling into Washington, where slavery was legal. It was still twenty years before the Civil War, and there was a high demand in the Deep South for slaves to work on cotton plantations.

It was not unheard of for people to be kidnapped and forced to work as slaves, particularly children. However, Northup still went. Expecting the trip to be short however, he did not tell his wife where he was going.

We don't know for sure, but it's possible that Northup was drugged by his two companions. He had some symptoms that would indicate poisoning by belladonna. They were able to subdue him. The men then sold Northup to a slave trader named James H. Birch for the sum of $650.

He was severely beaten, and then presented as a slave from Georgia. Northup was first held in a slave pen, and then shipped by sea to New Orleans. Along the way, Northup and his fellow captives caught smallpox, and one man died during the trip.

Upon arrival at New Orleans, Birch's partner Theophilus Freeman sold him to a preacher who owned a small farm in northern Louisiana. While there, Northup was able to convince an English sailor to send word to the son of the man who had freed his father, Henry Northup, now a lawyer. The two had been childhood friends. Although the state of New York had passed laws providing assistance to aid in the recovery of free men who were kidnapped and taken out of state, the lawyer could do nothing without knowing Northup's location.

Meanwhile, Northup found Ford to be a good man who was considerate of his slaves, however this did not mean he accepted his lot. Despite having no access to writing paper, and being under constant watch, he continued to try to get word out to his family and friends.

Northup did good work for Ford over the years, inventing several new systems to transport lumber more efficiently. However in 1842, Ford found him-self in financial stress, and sold Northup, along with eighteen other slaves. A man named John M. Tibaut, who worked for Ford, bought Northup and set him to work for his business on construction of Ford's plantation. He could not afford the full purchase price, and so Ford held a $400 chattel mortgage on Northup.

Unlike Ford, Tibaut was not a fair man, and regularly beat his slaves for little or no reason. Once, when he was attacked, Northup fought back and Tibaut was severely injured. Becoming enraged, he recruited two friends to lynch Northup.

Thankfully, they were interrupted by Ford's overseer, who prevented them from killing Northup, telling them to remember that Tibaut still owed Ford a debt for the slave. However, Northup was still left bound and noosed for hours until Ford returned and cut him down.

Tibaut continued to hold a grudge against Northup, and attempted to kill him again at a later time. He swung an axe at Northup, but Northup was again able to defend himself. Northup strangled Tibaut until he was unconscious, and then ran and made his way back to Ford.

At this point, Ford convinced Tibault to lease Northup out instead of using him directly. After a few weeks of this arrangement, Tibault sold Northup to a man named Edwin Epps. Epps would end up holding Northup as a slave for nearly ten years.

Epps was also a cruel man, who whipped slaves daily for not making quota, and also raped a female slave. In 1852 a man named Samuel Bass came to work for Epps. Northup overheard Bass talk of his abolitionist views, and decided to try to confide in the man. He told Bass his real name and origins.

Bass mailed letters written by Northup, as well as several of his own, to Northup's friends, telling them of his location. This was done at great personal risk to Bass, both from locals and also the Fugitive Slave Law Act of 1850, which had increased federal penalties for assisting a slave to escape.

Investigation:
Bass' letters eventually reached Cephas Parker and William Perry, who were storekeepers in Saratoga. They in turn contacted Henry Northup, who contacted the New York Governor, who then took up the case. However, Bass had been deliberately vague in his letters, should they fall into the wrong hands, not giving away Northup's precise location.

Before they could act, they also had to find documentation proving that Northup was a free man and citizen of New York State. They did not contact Northup while all this was ongoing, in fear of alerting Epps, and so Northup had no idea whether anyone had received his plea for help.

Eventually on January 1st, 1853, Henry Northup had completed the paperwork, found Bass (who had left the area) and confirmed where Northup was located. When confronted with the evidence that Northup was a free man, Epps at first demanded to know why Northup had not told him when he bought him.

It was later revealed that had Epps known that people were coming to free Northup, Epps would have ensured he never left alive. He also threatened to kill the man who had revealed the truth of the situation, but did not know of Bass's true identity. After finally convincing Epps to avoid contesting the papers, four months after he originally met with Bass, Northup was again a free man.

Northup was one of few free black people to regain their freedom after being sold into slavery. He filed a legal complaint against the man who had first enslaved him, and also sued Birch and the other men involved in Washington D.C.

Birch was arrested, but ironically Northup could not testify against him, as laws prevented a black man from testifying in court. Birch was found not guilty, and he then demanded that charges be filed against Northup for trying to defraud him. He eventually withdrew the charge after Northup showed he was eager to fight the charge rather than giving in.

Later that same year Northup wrote and published his now famous memoir, *Twelve Years a Slave*. It sold 30,000 copies in three years. From the book's publicity, a county court judge from Fonda, New York, named Thaddeus St. John, remembered seeing two friends of his in the company of a black man, who then disappeared at the same time that his old friends had suddenly come into a large amount of money.

They were identified as the men who had kidnapped Northup, and were arrested. This time Northup could testify, however because of a fight over jurisdiction, after more than two years of appeals the case failed to continue. No further legal action was taken against the men.

Northup rejoined his family, and by 1855 was living with his daughter's family in Warren County, New York. He was working as a carpenter and became active in abolitionist movements. This is where the second mystery of his life, the one that remains unsolved today, occurred.

In 1858 rumors were rife as to Northup's whereabouts. Newspapers reported that he had once again been sold into slavery. Around the same time, even Henry Northup is believed to have said Northup had been kidnapped in Canada. Northup was booked in to do a series of lectures on slavery in Ontario in 1857, but a wildly hostile crowd provontod him from spcaking. This is the last documented evidence of anything to do with the whereabouts of Solomon Northup.

Over time, many of his friends and associates were quoted as believing he had been kidnapped or killed, but all quoted different locations and times. Henry Northup's nephew wrote that Northup had been lecturing in Boston when he disappeared, where he also visited the son of a Methodist minister sometime after January 1863.

We do not know the exact date, only that it was after Lincoln's Emancipation Proclamation. The minister, Rev. Smith, had been helping fugitive slaves escape on the Underground Railroad.

Northup was not listed on the 1860 Census, though other members of his family were, including his wife. She is listed as married. However, in 1876 her own death notice reported that she was widowed. One of her obituary notices spoke badly of Northup, but talked of him as though he was still alive.

Some therefore believe that he died of natural causes before or after his wife, and he was never kidnapped, stating he was likely too old in the 1850's to be of any interest to slave traders. We know no more – not where he lived or when and how he died. After documenting and making public such an amazing period of his life, Solomon Northup simply disappeared and was never heard from again.

Current Status:
21st Century historians have been tracking what happened to Northup after his release for over a decade. David Fiske, a retired New York State librarian, joined with Clifford Brown (political professor) and Rachel Seligman (exhibition curator) and put together *The Complete Story of the Author of Twelve Years a Slave*.

They believe that Northup was almost certainly involved in the Underground Railroad after he found his own freedom. We know that he also became a prolific public speaker and owned property in Glens Falls, New York.

However, in 1854 he suffered financial worries, and his property was foreclosed on. Other creditors also won judgments over Northup. However, the historians involved in the project do not believe that he was killed, either as revenge by the men who kidnapped him, or that he was sold into slavery again. They believe that it's more likely that he simply became destitute and had given up, deciding to disappear from friends and family. Perhaps he died as a pauper and was buried in a potter's field.

It's very likely that at the time of his death the country was being ripped apart by civil war, and few may have taken the time to properly identify and bury an unidentified and destitute black man. However, despite checking cemeteries around Saratoga and other places in upstate New York, no death records matching Northup have ever been found.

Northup always did have a great sense of adventure, and so in the end, perhaps he went out West to try to strike it rich, reinventing himself with a new identity. For all the research, both at the time and now with the popularity of the movie release, it's unlikely we will ever know for sure.

The Heiress Went Shopping: Dorothy Arnold

Missing Person: Dorothy Arnold
Date: December 12th, 1910
Last Known Location: New York City

Backstory:
Dorothy Harriet Camille Arnold was born to a privileged life on July 1st, 1885. The second of four children, her father was a perfume importer named Francis Rose Arnold and her mother was named Mary Martha Parks Samuel Arnold. Arnold had an older brother, and two younger siblings, and was also the niece of a magistrate who would go on to become an Associate Justice of the Supreme Court, Rufus Wheeler Peckham.

The family was listed on the *Social Register*, a directory of names and addresses of American families who were considered the social elite. Arnold went to private girl's school, and then graduated from Bryn Mawr College with a major in literature and language.

After graduating from college, Arnold lived with her family on East 78th Street. She had a desire to start a career as a writer. Just two months before the fateful day, she was turned down by her father when she asked to live on her own in an apartment in Greenwich Village to concentrate on her writing.

After being teased by her family and friends over rejections she received, Arnold kept her career aspirations mostly private. She never did manage to have anything accepted for publication.

On The Day In Question:
December 12th, 1910 started like any other day. Arnold left to go shopping. She was intending to buy a new dress to wear to her younger sister's upcoming social debut. She is

reported to have had approximately $30 in cash on her person, a sum equivalent to well over $1,000 today.

Arnold first walked from 79th Street down to the corner of 5th Avenue and 27th Street, where she charged a half-pound box of chocolates to her account at the store Park & Tilford. She then visited a bookstore, where she purchased a book and also ran into her friend Gladys King. After a short chat, King excused her self and left to meet her mother for lunch. King later reported seeing Arnold for the last time on 27th Street just before 2pm.

Arnold never returned home that day, and by dinner her family was becoming worried. It was most unlike her to miss a meal without informing her family. They began calling Arnold's friends, but no one reported seeing her that day.

Shortly after midnight a friend named Elise Henry telephoned the home to ask if Arnold had returned. Curiously, she was allegedly informed by Arnold's mother that she was home and had gone to bed with a headache, and so was unable to speak on the phone.

Investigation:
From the beginning, the investigation into Arnold's disappearance was delayed. Fearing social embarrassment and unwanted attention from the media, her family did not report her as missing to the police for weeks.

They did however contact the family lawyer, John S. Keith, the morning after her disappearance. He visited the home and searched Arnold's room. He reported that all her clothes and personal belongings were still present.

He also found personal letters with foreign postmarks and two folders for transatlantic steamers on her desk. Lastly he discovered burned papers in her fireplace. He assumed that they were the remains of her failed publishing attempts.

From there, Keith searched hospitals, jails and morgues all over New York City. He repeated the same searches in Philadelphia and Boston, but no trace of Arnold was found. By this time weeks had passed, and Keith suggested that the family hire the famous Pinkerton detectives to investigate the case. They were hired, and the agency's first action was to send out circulars to area police stations, offering a $1,000 reward for her return.

The detectives repeated the same searches as Keith, and also questioned Arnold's friends and family. Everyone denied seeing her or having any knowledge of her whereabouts. After finding the steam liner brochures, the investigators decided she may have travelled to Europe with an unknown man to elope.

They ordered agents overseas to search steamers arriving from New York, but Arnold was not found to be among any of the passengers. Initially several young women matching her physical description were found, but none were definitively identified as Arnold.

By this time, Arnold's family was finally convinced to officially involve the police. The police's first advice was to hold a press conference, but her family refused. Finally, on January 25th, nearly six weeks after her disappearance, the family relented and a press conference was held by her father. At the time, he expressed his belief that she had been killed in Central Park on her way home, and her body disposed of in a reservoir.

There were again rumors that Arnold had run away from home with a man as her parents wouldn't let her date. Francis Arnold however refuted this claim, saying he would have been glad to allow Arnold to associate with a young man "…of brains and position", but that he did not approve of men who "…had nothing to do".

Reporters soon surmised that this was a reference to a man named George Griscom Jr., a man with whom Arnold had been linked. He was unmarried at forty-two, and came from a wealthy family in Pittsburgh.

According to reports, Arnold had earlier lied to her parents and visited him for a week, pawning $500 worth of jewels to pay for the expenses of the week. They had forbidden the relationship, but it's reported that Arnold still stayed in touch with Griscom anyway.

At the time of her disappearance, Griscom was located in Naples, where he was vacationing. He contacted the Arnold family by telegram and denied any knowledge of Arnold's whereabouts or disappearance. During January, Arnold's mother and brother travelled together to Italy to attempt to forcibly interrogate Griscom, but they were not successful.

Griscom however did turn over personal letters from Arnold in which she mentioned depression at her rejections as a writer, and on his return to the USA, invested thousands of dollars of his own money into the search, running ads in major newspapers.

Immediately after the press conference, investigators began receiving phone calls from all over the country reporting sightings of Arnold. None proved successful. The family also received two ransom notes, but they too were proven false. By the end of January, the police decided that Arnold was alive and would return home when she wanted to.

Conversely her family believed her dead, and still believed that her body had been disposed of in a reservoir. Police dismissed this as the temperature on the day of Arnold's disappearance meant the reservoir was frozen solid. Despite this, the park was still searched however, and again in the spring when the water thawed, but no evidence was ever found.

Current Status:
To this day, many theories and rumors persist regarding the disappearance of Dorothy Arnold. One hypothesis was that she had slipped and injured her head, forgetting who she was. However, no women matching her description with head injuries were ever found in local hospitals.

Other theories that she was drugged or abducted were dismissed as she had been last seen on a busy street. Her friend Griscom suggested suicide over her failed career, and some members of her family also believed that she killed herself, but rather over Griscom himself. It was discovered by the press that Griscom's cousin had also committed suicide after he was forbidden to marry an English governess, which helped encourage the rumors.

In early February Arnold's family received a postcard with a New York City postmark that read only "I am safe" and was signed "Dorothy". The writing was deemed a match to Arnold's, but Francis Arnold believed that someone copied his daughter's handwriting from samples in the newspaper, and the card was a fake.

Shortly after, the police reported that they were ceasing the investigation, seventy-five days after Arnold's initial disappearance. While they stopped looking for new leads, they still investigated reported sightings when they came in. Nothing ever lead to finding Arnold, or what happened to her.

In early April 1916, an illegal abortion clinic in Pennsylvania was raided after several women from the area went missing after visiting the clinic. A doctor there testified that Arnold had attended the clinic and died after complications from an abortion. He claimed her body was then burned in the clinic's furnace.

Rumors that Arnold had become pregnant out of wedlock had already existed, but perhaps these were just the product of an extremely 'proper' society, rather than based in any fact. The doctor's pronouncement however, was seen by many as confirmation of the rumors. Her family, of course, denied the allegations completely.

Perhaps 'inspired' by the resurgence of the case in the media, in late April 1916 a man named Edward Glennoris, who was already in jail after being convicted of attempted extortion, claimed that he had been paid $250 to bury the body of a woman back in December 1910, when Arnold had disappeared.

He claimed that a man named 'Little Louie' had hired him to drive a woman from a home in New Rochelle to West Point, both in New York. At the home they were met with two more men, one of which Glennoris claimed met the description of Griscom. The other was named only 'Doc'. They loaded a woman, who was at the time unconscious, into the car, and Glennoris drove her to a house in Weekawken, New Jersey.

Glennoris was reportedly informed during the drive that the woman's name was Dorothy Arnold, and he later was able to identify a signet ring that matched one she owned. The next day, Little Louie contacted him again and told him to return to the home in New Jersey to 'finish the job'. When he arrived, he found the woman dead, and was informed by Doc that she had died during an operation in the home.

They wrapped her in a sheet and Glennoris claimed he and Little Louie drove the body back to New Rochelle and buried her in the cellar of the home. Police investigated and dug up the cellar in several homes, but found no evidence of any human remains.

Occasional sighting reports continued over the years. It was not until 1921 that the case again garnered attention. This time, Captain John H. Ayers of the Bureau of Missing Persons was quoted as saying that the Bureau knew what happened to Arnold, but would not reveal to the public if she were dead or alive.

The next day however, he claimed to have been misquoted. The family's official position was that she had committed suicide, devastated from the failure of her writing career.

Arnold's family is reported to have spent $250,000 trying to find her. Until the day he died, her father believed she had been kidnapped and murdered way back on the day she originally disappeared. Conversely, her mother believed her to be alive, and went to her own grave with this belief intact.

To this day, not a single trace of Dorothy Arnold has ever been found. Did she run away with a wealthy boyfriend, or simply could not stand the stress of failing at her life's dream, and being ridiculed for it by her family?

Perhaps she rebelled against her father's refusal for her to move out of the family home and decided the only way she was going to be able to live her own life was to disappear and start again. Whatever happened to her, it's clear that if her disappearance was planned by Arnold herself, she kept it extremely private, as even her own family never came to a consensus on what they believed happened to her, and disagreed to the day of their own deaths.

Lost in the Jungle: Percy Fawcet, Jack Fawcet, Jack's Friend

Missing Persons: Percy Fawcett, Jack Fawcet, Jack's Friend
Date: Sometime after May 29th,1925
Last Known Location: The jungles of Brazil

Backstory:
Percy Fawcett was born Percival Harrison Fawcett on August 18th, 1867, to parents Edward Boyd Fawcett and Myra Elizabeth. His father was born in India, and was a Fellow of the Royal Geographic Society. Adventure ran in the family, and his older brother, Edward was a mountain climber and author of adventure novels.

Fawcett was educated at Newton Abbot Proprietary College, and received a commission into the Royal Artillery in 1886. He served at Ceylon (now Sri Lanka), where he first met his wife, Nina Agnes Paterson.

They married in January 1901, and they had two sons, Brian and Jack. The same year as he married, Fawcett also joined the Royal Geographic Society himself, continuing an interest in surveying and map making. This led him to work for the British Secret Service in North Africa. Here, he made friends with H. Rider Haggard and Arthur Conan Doyle.

Fawcett went on an expedition to South America in 1906, where he went to Brazil to map a jungle filled area on the border of Argentina, under the request of the Royal Geographic Society.

Fawcett made several amazing claims of discoveries while on the expedition, including shooting a 62 ft. anaconda, and seeing other strange animals. He was widely ridiculed by the scientific community regarding the claims.

Between 1906 and 1924, Fawcett continued to visit South America and made seven different expeditions. He is reported as being mostly patient and polite to the natives, as well as bringing gifts, and got along well with them. His claims of amazing animals continued, and based on research at some point he formulated an idea about a Lost City in Brazil.

However, this occurred around the time of the start of World War I, and so Fawcett returned to Britain and underwent active military service. Despite being nearly fifty years old, he led an artillery brigade. After the war was over, he returned to Brazil.

On The Day In Question:
In 1925, funded by a group based in London, Fawcett returned once again to Brazil, this time also bringing his son, Jack, along with Jack's friend. Through his studies of legends and historical records, he was convinced that there was a lost city somewhere in a region named Mato Grosso. Perhaps foreshadowing what was to come, he insisted that if his party failed to return that no one was to go in after them, lest they suffer the same fate.

With many years of expeditions behind him, Fawcett's party certainly were not inexperienced travelers, and they were also well outfitted and prepared with canned food, guns, navigation devices, and flares. All members of the party were in good health, and their personal relationships ensured loyalty.

Fawcett believed traveling with only his son and his son's good friend would lessen the attention of native tribes, being less risky than traveling with a larger party. Some tribes, it was reported, were now hostile to explorers.

Fawcett set out from Cuiaba on April 20th, 1925. Along with his companions, he traveled with two Brazilian laborers. He also took along two horses, two dogs, and eight mules. He wrote a letter to his wife on May 29th, reporting he was entering previously uncharted territory taking only Jack and his friend along.

The letter, written from Dead Horse Camp, a previous camp of Fawcett's with a known location, showed Fawcett to be generally in good spirits. He wrote that his wife "…need have no fear of any failure…" After that letter, she, nor anyone else, ever heard from Fawcett or his traveling companions again.

Investigation:
Fawcett and his group were last officially sighted by the Kalapalo Indians, whom many believe killed the group.

Although nothing was ever recorded officially, an oral story passed down through generations of the Kalapalo Indians talks of the arrival of three explorers who went east, and after five days the tribe noticed they were no longer making campfires.

They believe that another violent Indian tribe killed them. Contradicting this story however, at their last confirmed sighting both Jack and his friend were ill and lame, and no proof they were murdered has ever been found.

Current Status:
Like any disappearance, there are many rumors surrounding the disappearance of Fawcett and his travelling companions. Despite his own wishes, over the following years several rescue missions were mounted.

None of them were ever successful, and found only more rumors and speculation, everything from the group being killed by wild animals to Fawcett losing his memory and becoming chief of a cannibal tribe. It seems as though he was right to ask that no one come after them. It's estimated that one hundred of his potential rescuers have died attempting to discover what happened to the group.

An expedition in 1951 uncovered human bones, and claims were made that they were Fawcett's remains. His remaining son Brian refused to accept this, and was criticized by Brazilian activist Orlando Villas-Boas for the denial, claiming that Brian Fawcett wanted only to make money from the mystery. However, later further analysis revealed that he was correct. The bones had no link to the Fawcett family.

Villas-Boas stated that Fawcett had lost most of the gifts they were bringing to the native tribes due to a mishap on the way. The party was gravely ill and was killed by the Kalapalo tribe. Another explorer who heard this story, a Danish man Arne Falk-Ronne, said that a member of the tribe had told him this was the truth.

Today, we are still no closer to a final answer on what happened to Fawcett and his companions. In 2004 a British newspaper reported that a television director, having studied Fawcett's private papers, thinks that he did not have any intention to return at all. Instead, he meant to form a commune out in the jungle. The same director used the research also in part as the preface of the play, AmaZonia.

The most likely explanation is that hostile natives killed Fawcett. However it's also possible that he and his party eventually became too ill to travel further and simply passed away. Perhaps one day their remains will eventually be found.

The Hungarian Train Killer: Szilveszter Matuska

Missing Person: Szilveszter Matuska
Date: Sometime in 1944
Last Known Location: Hungary

Backstory:
Szilveszter Matuska was born on January 29th, 1892 in Serbia. Little is known about his childhood. We do know that he was a former officer of the Austro-Hungarian army. He first came to public attention in October 1931, when he was arrested for arranging the derailment of several trains.

The first of his successes was with the derailment of the Berlin-Basel express, just south of Berlin in August 1931. Although no one was killed, many were injured. A defaced Nazi newspaper was found at the scene, along with other evidence that lead to the belief that the crime was politically motivated. At the time, no one knew who was responsible, and a bounty of 100,000 reichsmark was placed.

Perhaps learning a few things the first time round, his second successful attempt at derailment (that we know of) was far more spectacular. The Vienna Express was crossing Biatorbagy Bridge near Budapest just after midnight on September 13th, 1931. Part of the bridge was blown up, and the train plunged into a ravine nearly 100 feet deep. Twenty-two people died, and another 120 were injured.

Matuska was discovered at the scene, but passed himself off as a passenger and was initially released. However, one month later, after investigators tracked him over three countries, he was arrested in Vienna, and soon confessed.

He was tried and convicted in Austria for two other unsuccessful attempts, before being extradited to Hungary. However, a condition was made on his extradition that he not be given the death penalty. He was found guilty and sentenced to death, but as per the agreement he was instead given life in prison.

On The Day In Question:
Matuska was imprisoned in Vac, a town in Hungary approximately 22 miles north of Budapest. However, he was not to remain there. In 1944, 13 years after the derailment, he escaped. No one knows how he managed the feat.

Investigation:
Matuska was never recaptured and no official sightings have ever been made. Given his background and the timing of his escape, rumors have circulated that he worked as an explosives expert during World War II.

Perhaps given his political leanings, rumors again surfaced that he was working on the communist side in the Korean War. No supporting evidence for these rumors has ever been found.

Current Status:
To this day, we are no wiser as to the true motivations for Mutuska's crimes. Evidence from the first crime seemed to indicate political involvement. At the trial however, Mutuska claimed to have been told to derail the train by God. He later claimed to enjoy the experience immensely, and that he orgasmed when the trains crashed.

Knowing such little details as to what became of him has not stopped Matuska appearing in popular culture. In 1990, he was the subject of a song by a punk/industrial band from Illinois named Lard. A Hungarian/German made for TV movie based on the case and named *The Train Killer* (in English) was released in 1983. Later still, in 1993, he was the subject of a Belgian artist's art installation.

A Lord Gone Mad: Lord Richard Lucan

Missing Person: Lord Lucan
Date: November 7th, 1974
Last Known Location: London, England

Backstory:

Lord Lucan was born as Richard John Bingham, the 7th Earl of Lucan, on the 18th of December 1934. Born into an aristocratic family, he was the eldest son of George Bingham (the 6th Earl of Lucan) and his wife Kaitlin Elizabeth Anne.

While the family was part of the social elite, scandal has been tied to the family for many generations, starting with Lord Lucan's great-great-grandfather, who had ordered the Charge of the Light Brigade in the Crimean War, which eventually caused the deaths of over 600 men.

Like many children in England, Lucan was evacuated because of World War II. Eventually, however even the English countryside was not seen as safe enough, the children eventually being sent all the way to America. Despite the war, the children still lived extremely comfortably while in the USA.

After his return to England, Lucan attended the prestigious school Eton, and went on to serve with the Coldstream Guards, a Foot Guard regiment of the British Army, in West Germany. He was an extremely charismatic man with tastes that met his station in life, and was even once considered for the role of James Bond. A tall man, he stood at 6 foot 4 inches, and was considered to be very handsome.

Lucan married Veronica Duncan in 1964, and they had three children. Just two months after the wedding, his father died and he became the new Earl of Lucan. The title came with a large inheritance and privileges.

It has been reported that after her children were born, Lady Lucan suffered from severe postnatal depression, even suffering from hallucinations at one point. She did seek help, but was wrongly diagnosed and the treatment did not work. It's said that Lord Lucan did try to help, and attempted to admit her to a hospital for psychiatric treatment, but she refused.

Unfortunately their marriage did not last, and in 1972 he moved out of the family home. An intense custody battle ensued, and Lucan lost. It was then that he allegedly became obsessed with regaining custody of his children, spying on his wife and recording her telephone conversations. He told friends that he believed she could not care for the children due to her mental illness, attempting to gain sole custody himself.

Around the same time his lifelong love of gambling got him into trouble. He had often lost more than he won and by this time in his life, along with the split and lengthy legal battles, his personal finances were under fire. Once he lost the custody battle, he began to drink heavily, and reportedly blamed his life's downward spiral on his wife.

On The Day In Question:
Veronica Lucan (Lady Lucan) had remained in the family home with the children, and hired a nanny, Sandra Rivett, a woman in her late twenties. On November 7th, 1974, Rivett went to make a pot of tea at around 8:55pm. Lady Lucan remained upstairs with the children, but when Rivett had not come back after approximately fifteen minutes, Lady Lucan started to worry, and went to check on her.

The home was six stories, and the kitchen, along with a breakfast room, was located in the basement. When she was still on the first floor, it caught Lady Lucan's attention that the basement light was switched off, even though

Rivett was supposed to be down there making tea. She tried to turn the light on but it didn't work.

Calling out to Rivett got no response. She went to check on some noises she had heard in the cloakroom, and it was here that she was suddenly and brutally attacked. Hit over the head repeatedly with a weighty object, she screamed and a strong voice told her to shut up. Lady Lucan had a small build, at barely 5ft 2 inches and 100 pounds, and her attacker was large.

He attempted to choke her, and then suffocate her and claw at her eyes. Lady Lucan however would not give up without a fight. She managed to grab onto her attacker's testicles and give them a hard squeeze. The attack temporarily ceased and she was able to escape.

Her home was only thirty yards away from a local pub, and Lady Lucan ran through the front door, screaming of the murder of her nanny and that the children had been left back at the house with her attacker. Despite her panic, no one in the pub rushed to the house. Instead, they notified the police. Lady Lucan collapsed and was taken to a hospital.

The police arrived at the home quickly, and a search found a pool of blood in the ground floor stairwell, however the three children were not harmed and were unaware of any trouble. A further search found the door to the basement had been left open, and a piece of 9-inch lead pipe was covered in blood.

More blood was found in the room, and the light bulb for the room had been deliberately removed. Also in the room was a canvas mailbag, and inside police found the bloody and beaten body of Rivett.

By midnight, police were on their way to Lord Lucan's apartment. He was gone.

Investigation:

By evening of the next day, police had interviewed Lady Lucan in the hospital. She was badly injured but alive. After recounting the circumstances surrounding to attack, she told police that she knew her attacker. Giving the police full details of the attack, she recounted that she was absolutely sure that the attacker had been her husband.

She reported that once she first incapacitated him, he had confessed to accidently killing Rivett in her place. Scared that he would still kill her, she agreed to cover for him and say that an unknown man had attacked.

She was told by her husband to take some sleeping pills, and she agreed if she first went to her bedroom upstairs. She reported that they both went upstairs and Frances, their eldest child who was still watching TV at the time, later recounted that she remembered seeing her mother with blood on her face.

Lady Lucan told Frances to go her room and told police that her husband then checked her injuries in the bathroom. He told her to lie on the bed, and then left to get towels to clean her. It was then she seized the opportunity and fled the house, running to the nearby pub.

Police searched Lord Lucan's apartment, and found that his keys and personal effects, including his passport, were all in place. They also found several address books, and so they began with calling the names in the books and interviewing Lucan's friends.

A woman named Susan Maxwell-Scott told police that Lucan had knocked at the front door at approximately 11:30pm that night. He had looked unkempt, and his pants were wet, looking like they had recently been scrubbed clean.

She invited him in, and he said that he had been passing by the family home when he saw Lady Lucan inside, involved in a struggle against a unknown man in the basement. He went inside himself and attempted to rescue her, but slipped in a puddle of blood.

He said that the man had fled on his arrival, and his wife then became hysterical, blaming him for the whole incident. He helped settle Lady Lucan and clean her wounds, but after she ran away from him, he was scared she would call police and he had decided to keep cover for a while.

According to Maxwell-Scott, Lucan had tried to call three other people – a friend named Madeleine Floorman, his mother, then Bill Shand Kydd, the husband of his sister-in-law. He may have also attempted to visit Floorman, but she had not answered the door.

Lucan's mother was told that there was a catastrophe back at the home, and asked if she could take the children back with her to her home. Trying again when he was at Maxwell-Scott's home, Lucan was still unable to reach Kydd, and so wrote him two letters.

The first expressed fear that Lady Lucan would do anything to see him accused, and that it would be too much to bear for his children to grow up thinking he had tried to kill their mother. He asked Kydd to take custody of the children. The second contained only financial information, informing him of an upcoming sale at Christies auction house, which would '*satisfy bank overdrafts*'.

Around 1:15am, Lucan left Maxwell-Scott's home driving a Ford Corsair, a car he had borrowed from a friend several weeks earlier. Three days after the initial attack, on November 10th, police investigators found the car abandoned around sixteen miles away, near Newhaven docks.

The Ford was covered in bloodstains, and a pipe made of lead and matching the pipe found at the scene of the crime was found inside the car. A notepad missing a piece of paper was also recovered. Michael Stoop, the car's owner, later also received mail from Lucan. It was written on the same paper as that in the notepad. In the letter, Lucan claimed that no one would ever believe his version of events, and for Michael to please tell his children that '*all I cared about was them.*'

A few reports from fishermen placed a man matching Lucan's description on the docks early in the morning of the 8th of November, but the sightings amounted to nothing and no other evidence was recovered at the scene. Lord Lucan had disappeared from the face of the earth.

It took a week after the attacks for a warrant to be issued for Lucan's arrest. Until then, police were unable to search his private property, and they have been criticized in this for giving Lucan the time he needed to disappear.

In July 1975, an inquest into Rivett's death was held. There was much debate as to whether Lady Lucan should be allowed to testify. The laws of the time only allowed a wife to testify against her husband if he was being charged with her own assault.

The coroner allowed her to testify, despite the fact Lucan was not charged officially, and Lady Lucan testified. Frances Lucan also corroborated her mother's story from her point of view. This time, she reported seeing her father in the house.

It was reported that Rivett had died choking on her own blood, and would have died quickly, within minutes of the attack.

Lucan's mother also testified, reporting that Lord Lucan had been incoherent when they spoke, but that he didn't go into details with her beyond asking her to go and get the children. Michael Stoop also testified that there had been no lead pipe in the car when he lent it to Lucan.

Although there was no DNA testing available at the time, a blood analysis forensic test was revealing. It found that Rivett's blood type (B) was mostly concentrated downstairs around the basement, and Lady Lucan's blood type (A) along the hallway. No blood was found in the cloakroom, where Lady Lucan had reported being attacked.

What caught investigator's interest was that the same blood type as Lady Lucan was discovered on the mailbag containing Rivett's body, and on the bloody pipe. Perhaps the attacker and Lady Lucan shared the same blood type? The pipe did not retain any hair from either woman, but hairs belonging to Lady Lucan were also in the car.

AB blood type stains were found on the letters sent to Kydd. However, it's possible these were formed if someone handling them had both Rivett's and Lady Lucan's blood on their hands. It was also found in the Ford, and on the ground floor hallway. Finally, only Rivett's blood was found outside in the garden, and in a man's bloody footprint leading out of the basement.

The same fibers were found in the car, the basement, bathroom sink, towel and the pipe. Investigators believe that the fibers came from the man who attacked both women. Together with the blood evidence, it proved that whoever it was that attacked that night had also been in the Corsair, the car that Lucan had been seen driving.

There was no evidence found at the home to suggest anyone had slipped over in a puddle of blood, as Lord Lucan had told his friend to explain his physical appearance. Police also tried to recreate Lucan's peering in at the basement window where he said he had seen the attack, but they found that the view was almost impossible to see unless you deliberately stooped low and peered in. Even then, only the last four stairs were visible, and with the light removed as on the night of the attack, visibility would have been practically none.

Therefore, it then came down to timing. Testimony by a doorman placed Lucan at the Clermont Club for dinner at approximately 8:45pm. He was wearing casual clothes, and was not unsettled at all.

Even if he left the club immediately, it would be difficult for him to be at the house by 9:00pm, let alone remove the light bulb and lay in wait. The timing was close enough however, that the club doorman being just ten minutes off would change everything, giving him enough time to commit the crime.

Although it does not hold the same weight as a conviction in criminal court, in just half an hour the coroner's jury found that Rivett's death was caused by murder by Lord Lucan.

Current Status:
Lucan's case has attracted worldwide attention, with whole websites devoted to the mystery and his supposed whereabouts. At first, many believed he took his own life off the docks, but an extensive search of the water did not find a body. At the same time, fourteen sniffer dogs tried to detect Lucan's scent on land in the area. They did not find a single trace.

Others wondered if he stowed aboard a ferry, and two fishermen did claim to see a man matching his appearance. Investigators even travelled to France and interviewed immigration officers, but found no one who had seen anyone matching Lucan's description.

Evidence from Interpol also suggested Lucan may have been in France. In 1975, a hotel owner reported that a guest who stayed often matched Lucan's description. Staff members identified him from a photograph, and said that he had hired a local girl for forty-five minutes a day, as many days as possible. It's therefore possible that she had been tasked with teaching Lucan French. The man in the hotel spoke fluent French.

Over the years, sightings have been reported from all over the world. Of particular interest were those from South Africa. Detectives discovered that the Lucan children spent much time there vacationing when they were adults. In 1995, a British newspaper published that Scotland Yard was convinced Lucan was alive and residing in Johannesburg. The children's travels were monitored, but nothing ever came to light that supported the theory.

Finally, in 1999 Lucan was himself declared officially dead. His estate, worth under £15,000, was released to executors. However this did not stop the sightings, most recently in Australia in May 2000.

Multiple books have been published about the case and the surrounding mystery. A former nanny for the couple, named Stefanja Sawicka, allegedly told authors writing a book about Lucan that he beat his wife, pushing her down the stairs, and attempting to strangle her on more than one occasion. Lady Lucan allegedly had told Sawicka that she feared for her life.

Other authors have claimed Lucan told his friends that he wanted to kill his wife, but they took his claims as nothing more than the ramblings of a drunken man.

Interestingly, naming Lord Lucan as the killer in the coroner's court was the last such verdict to ever be given. Based on this very hearing, just one month later, a bill was passed banning the coroner's court from naming a murderer.

The Cadet Went Missing: Richard Cox

Missing Person: Richard Colvin Cox
Date: January 14th, 1950
Last Known Location: West Point Academy

Backstory:

Richard Colvin Cox was born on July 25, 1928 in Mansfield, Ohio. He graduated high school in 1946, and the following year served in the Sixth Constabulary Regiment of the U.S. Army. He was stationed in Coburg, Germany, in the intelligence section of the Company Headquarters.

The office was located near the newly formed borders between East and West Germany, and according to military journalists, the Constabulary's job was to man border posts and run patrols. The soldiers were watched by East German and Soviet troops, armed heavily and observing them through binoculars, standing less than a football field away.

Serving with Cox was an army official known only as "George." Although he was to play a vital role in what was to come, we know little more about him. A short time later, in 1947, Cox applied for an appointment to West Point. He arrived in January of 1948.

By all accounts, Cox was a devoted son and fiancée, engaged to a woman named Betty Timmons, whom he was planning to marry after his graduation from West Point. He was a smart man, achieving excellent grades in his classes, and there was no indication there was anything in his life that would cause him to simply walk away from it all.

On The Day In Question:

On Saturday, January 7th, 1950 a classmate of Cox's, Peter Hains, received a call. Hains was the Charge of

Quarters in the cadet company, and he answered the incoming calls for all of the company members. At 4:45pm a call came in for Cox.

The caller was "rough and patronizing", and when he was told that Cox was not available, Hains was informed to simply tell him when he returned that George had called. According to George, he and Cox had served together in Germany and Cox would know who he was. George was stateside, and wanted to catch up over dinner.

Later that evening, Cox returned and got the message. He signed the departure book, and made a note that he was having dinner off-campus. He was met by George in the visitor's area, and the pair sat in George's car (parked on campus) and drank whisky together. A short while later, Cox signed back in, had a shower, and went to bed, presumably to sleep off any effects from the alcohol.

It was later discovered that at a time unknown, Cox changed the listing in the departure log to be an hour earlier, to make it appear as though he been present for the cadet supper formation at 6:30pm. This detail was not discovered until two years later. At the time, nobody noticed.

On January 8th, George visited again. This time, no one noticed Cox drinking, and neither did he admit to having any this time. Over the next few days, Cox did mention having a visitor, but never named him. Cox claimed he was a former Army Ranger, and that his friend had a few brutal stories from the war he liked to tell, including that he had gotten a German girl pregnant and then murdered her before she could have the baby.

On January 14th, 1950 at approximately 6:00pm, George visited again and this time the two men left the academy grounds. After that, Richard Colvin Cox was never seen again. The mysterious 'George' has never been identified.

Investigation:

Interviews with Cox's roommates reported that Cox seemed upset when he returned from his first meeting, saying that George was the last guy he ever expected to see again. He said he had to agree to meet with him again the next day before George would let him leave that first time.

Cox then fell asleep for a few moments, before being startled awake, at which point he allegedly called out "Alles ist Kaput!" which is German for *all is finished*. However, when interviewed later, his roommates claimed they were not entirely sure exactly what Cox had said.

Cox had acted normally on his final day at the academy. He undertook his normal duties until 2:00pm, when everyone was then freed for the weekend. He watched a basketball game and then departed for dinner and into oblivion.

When Cox did not return, a large-scale manhunt was launched. Teams of multiple men walked at arms length through the academy grounds, all 15,000 acres. Both the pond and the reservoir were drained, but they found nothing. From there, officials at West Point notified the FBI, the army criminal division and both the New York State and City Police.

They widened the search, including every state in the USA, Canada, and even into Germany. Investigators probed every aspect of both Cox and his relative's lives, but nothing was ever found to help explain his disappearance.

The search of Cox's room found $60 cash, $25 in checks, and his watch. His civilian clothing was all still hanging in his cupboard. Nothing was missing to indicate that he'd planned an extended time away. His cadet records were exemplary, showing that Cox was in the upper third of his class, and ranked first in the company for military aptitude. No one had any idea where or why he had disappeared.

Current Status:
Many believe that Cox may have known something about black market or illegal activity in Germany. Something that was important enough to kill for. Howovor, his life in Germany was examined during the investigation, and no suspicious circumstances or connections were noted.

Another rumor speculated if he may have had an early glimpse into what would become the West Point cribbing scandal. In 1951, West Point would often give the exact same tests to two academic groups who had classes on different days. It was revealed that cadets were sharing information as to what was found on the tests between each other. West Point has a strict honor code, and the revelation was a massive scandal. Did Cox have early knowledge of the scandal from someone who hadn't wanted it to get out?

Some postured that he had been affected by amnesia or been in an accident and simply wandered off. But, unlike a civilian, a West Point cadet in full dress uniform would have been quickly recognized. Cox's history and record also made going AWOL unlikely. Before George came back on the scene he was considered an exemplary cadet. He also could have simply resigned from the academy if he felt so strongly about leaving as to fake his own disappearance.

Investigators probed into Cox's outfit in Germany and looked at every man with a first or last name of George, or even those that may have sounded like it. Each of the men were able to prove they were nowhere near West Point on the day Cox disappeared.

To this day, Cox is the only West Point cadet that has ever vanished and never been found – before or since the day he stepped out to dinner and into history

An Heir Lost at Sea: Michael Rockefeller

Missing Person: Michael Rockefeller
Date: November 18th, 1961
Last Known Location: New Guinea

Backstory:
Michael Rockefeller was the youngest child of Nelson and Mary Rockefeller, and a member of a family considered one of the most powerful in the United States. He and his twin sister Mary were the youngest of five children. He had sandy hair, and a thin build.

Rockefeller was raised in extreme privilege; the family had many servants, he attended first class private schools, and he travelled internationally often.

Nelson Rockefeller's own mother was highly interested in art, a passion she shared with her children. He started his own art collection when he was still young, and had a particular interest in primitive and native art.

His interest included the native populations of Oceania – part of the world that includes Australia, Polynesia, New Zealand, and New Guinea. He passed that interest on to Michael.

Despite his upbringing, Rockefeller was a hard worker and was determined to make his own way in life. He was determined to experience all that life had to offer, and work his own way up. He worked as everything from a grocery bagger to livestock herder on a family ranch. Family described him as someone who loved beautiful things and was enthusiastic in everything that he did, intrigued by the unexplored.

Rockefeller was a 'shoo in' for Harvard, due to family donations, but he worked hard and graduated cum laude in

1960 with a degree in English. There was one perk of being a Rockefeller that Michael did engage in.

The family wealth meant that he did not have to immediately find a job upon graduating. He planned on returning to study at some point, but upon graduation he was considering a trip to South America to collect art. He also had a six-month commitment to the U.S. Army Reserve.

Around that time he learned from a roommate that a Harvard professor named Robert Gardner, was planning a research trip to New Guinea. Gardner specialized in filming primitive cultures, and Rockefeller gave a pitch to be included on the trip. He pledged to pay his own way, and was invited along as a sound recorder and photographer.

Just weeks after he finished his Army Reserve training, Rockefeller left for New Guinea. At the time, New Guinea was a territory of the Netherlands, and commonly known as Dutch New Guinea.

The trip was focusing on the Ndani tribe that lived in a mountainous interior of the island. However on the way, they stopped in the colonial capital, where Dutch government authorities gave them an introduction to native handcrafts. Gardner and the group then continued on to film the Ndani people.

It's here that we have some of the last photos of Rockefeller. Unlike his polished, clean- shaven look in his family portraits, he had a full beard and was dressed in khakis and sneakers. He was photographed with natives, who apart from penises covered in gourds, were completely naked.

During their visit, the group recorded graphic violence between the tribesmen. They also collected samples of their weapons and tools. Rockefeller took photographs documenting the sometimes serious injuries caused by battles between nearby villages. Although they later denied it, the group was accused by Dutch authorities of inciting the fights.

As their visit continued, Rockefeller made plans to visit another tribe, the Asmat, on the southwest coast. The tribe had infrequent contact with the outside world, and they were also reputed to be very fierce and unfriendly. However, Gardner was full of descriptions of their primitive art, and Rockefeller wanted to see it.

He left the group in late June and embarked on his side trip. He would return on July 10th, stating no problems with the tribe. He had already bartered with the Asmat tribe for some of their art, and he was dreaming of a show at his father's museum. He also bartered commissions for other pieces, and had plans to return to collect them at a later date.

Upon return to the USA at the start of September, Rockefeller found out his parents were planning to divorce. He threw himself into his art exhibition project by day, and at night compiled research and edited his journal notes from the trip.

He made plans to visit as many New Guinea villages as possible, many only accessible by boat down the river, and to store his collection at a base camp. Required government approval was quickly given for the venture, thanks to his family connections.

On The Day In Question:
Rockefeller returned to New Guinea in September, barely two weeks after his original arrival home. He was assigned a guide from the Dutch government, Rene Wassink. It has since been noted that Wassink was an unusual choice, as he was not a native bushman but a Dutch anthropologist.

The pair were also given a strange boat to use for their travels, a makeshift catamaran that had been adapted from a design used for water patrols. They were allegedly warned that the boat was not suitable for use in open seas, as it was top heavy. They were also warned to not overload it, and to avoid the mouth of the Eilanden River, due to its strong tidal surges.

Rockefeller set out with Wassink in mid-October, and they quickly visited dozens of villages. Catholic priests, who worked among the Asmat as missionaries often introduced them. His letters home were full of enthusiasm, and included details of his collected pieces, including painted heads.

Later, some Dutch officials would reveal they were concerned Rockefeller had created a market for the heads that would lead to bloodshed. The goods he bartered for each head were highly valuable, more than he bartered for his whole boat. Rockefeller was again allegedly informed of their concerns, but if the conversation did take place, it is not mentioned in any of his letters or journal entries.

Rockefeller's notes talked about their diet (spam, rice, and corned beef), and how they bathed in the river and slept wrapped in bug nets. He did talk about problems they were having with their boat, noting that it was unstable and sometimes made crossing the river dangerous. His letters home talked about his hopes to be home by Christmas, and how much he was enjoying his trip.

In the final days, Rockefeller and Wassink made a tribe to visit a tribe of about 1,500 people in Astj. When they were going to leave, it's noted that a police official told them that their boat was dangerously overloaded, and it would have to be lightened before they could leave.

Once the official had moved on however, Rockefeller left without making a single change to the cargo. On board the boat were Rockefeller, Wassink, and two local Asmat teenagers. It was noon on November 18th, 1961.

As reported later by Wassink, the two Asmat boys encouraged Rockefeller to speed along the coast, passing the mouth of the Eilanden River that they were warned to avoid. At 2:15pm, the boat entered the water where the river flowed into the seas and a wave came over the stern. It swamped the hulls and cut the engine.

The boat was sinking, and at the same time they were being further swept out to sea by the surge. The boys, both afraid, said they would swim to shore. Each took a jerrican, emptied it, and left, using it as a life buoy. They promised they would send help from shore.

The boat continued to push further out to sea, and just before dark another wave capsized the vessel completely. Rockefeller and Wassink were now clinging to an empty hull. The sun had gone down, and they were cold, wet, and being further dragged out to sea. Help did not arrive, and they spent a long night out in the water.

As dawn broke over the horizon, and help had still not arrived, the pair started to debate their options. They could just make out land in the distances, and they estimated it to be approximately 4-7 miles away. Later, official estimates would put them more like 11 miles out.

They tried to paddle the boat with driftwood, but that did not work. Rockefeller, a strong swimmer himself, argued that they had no way of knowing if the Asmat teens were coming back with help, and he should swim for it himself. Wassink tried to talk him out of it, but in the end Rockefeller emptied two more cans for himself and left, saying "I think I can make it."

He was never seen again.

Investigation:

As it turned out, the two Asmat boys swam for over five hours to shore, and did then alert authorities for help. Within hours of being notified, the government had three planes and twelve boats looking for the pair. Wassink was located alone at 4:00pm and rescued by the Royal Netherlands Navy.

At this time, Rockefeller's parents were notified he was missing. His father and twin sister, along with a large group of journalists, flew immediately to New Guinea. Nelson Rockefeller worked closely with the government in co-coordinating the search, and took several trips himself by airplane and by sea to the area where Rockefeller was last seen. He was quoted as saying that he had complete confidence in his son's stamina and resourcefulness.

Thousands of people were involved in the search, and every boat and plane at the government's disposal was used. Australia also added dozens of air and watercraft of their own. Although hampered by lack of modern communications available at the time, plus the thick jungle that covered much of the terrain, the search has been called the greatest in the island's history.

After ten days of searching, not a single trace of Michael Rockefeller or evidence to support he had survived, was found. The ever-pragmatic Nelson Rockefeller held a press conference stating that his son had been lost at sea and the search was called off.

After accepting a condolences call from President Kennedy, he left the country and returned home. On his arrival home, he immediately spoke to journalists, delivering a poignant and touching tribute to his son, stating that he had never been happier than in the last eight months on his trip.

Current Status:

Wassink believed that Rockefeller never survived his attempt to swim back to shore. The time he left meant he would have been swimming against the tide, making even a short swim extremely difficult. Although Wassink himself was never directly blamed, many blamed the Dutch government for assigning someone so inexperienced as Rockefeller's guide.

Meanwhile, media across the globe published sensational stories of what may have happened to him, many involve him being eaten by a shark or crocodile.

Over time, individuals have reported that Rockefeller had either 'gone native' himself, or was being held captive by a native tribe. Another rather gruesome claim to emerge was that he was himself killed by a tribe, and then cannibalized.

A Dutch Catholic Priest named Rev. Gerald Zegwaard believed that Rockefeller could have been killed by an aggrieved tribesman for revenge. In 1958, white police had killed five members of a particular tribe located not far from where Rockefeller disappeared. Perhaps he was killed in retaliation for the killings by the 'white tribe'.

Both the murder and the cannibalism theories have also attracted rumors that these theories may be true, and have been covered up by the Dutch government. There is no evidence to support either one, however there is also no evidence to definitively point to a drowning at sea. We simply do not know where Michael Rockefeller met his demise.

Within two years of his disappearance, New Guinea was given back to Indonesia. The eastern half of the country won independence in 1975 and is now called Papua New Guinea. Both halves of the island are now much more heavily mapped.

Yet, even as late as 2005 US magazines ran stories about guided tours to 'first contact' visits with primitives. Many Asmat crafts and artifacts from Rockefeller's collection are still on display in the Metropolitan Museum of Art. A wing of primitive art is named in his honor.

Three Children Vanished: Jane, Arnna & Grant Beaumont

Missing Persons: Jane, Arnna & Grant Beaumont
Date: January 26th, 1966
Last Known Location: Glenelg, South Australia.

Backstory:

Jane (aged 9), Arnna (age 7) and Grant (4) lived with their parents, Jim and Nancy Beaumont, in Somerton Park, a suburb of Adelaide in South Australia. The family lived near Glenelg, a popular beachside suburb, and the children loved to visit the local beaches.

On The Day In Question:

Summers in Australia are hot, and January 26th, 1966 in Adelaide was no exception. The temperature that day was due to peak at over 104 degrees. January 26th is Australia Day, a national holiday in Australia (similar to the 4th of July in the US), and many families flocked to the beach to escape the heat.

The Beaumont children often caught the bus for a five-minute ride to the beach on their own. In fact, they had done a similar trip just the day before. Their father, Jim, considered going with his children to the beach that day.

However, even with a holiday he thought that he should go into work. His trip to work was a two-hour commute. Jane was considered a mature child, and their parents believed she was responsible enough to look after her younger siblings on her own.

The bus stop was less than 100 yards from their home, and the bus driver, Mr. I. D. Monroe confirmed that the children were on his bus. A female passenger also later identified them, including confirming clothing they were wearing and belongings the children had with them.

The children left the bus at approximately 10:15am, at a stop just a short walk to the beach. The entire trip was so short that the children could have ridden their bikes, but given the heat of the day, their mother decided a bus trip was a better idea.

From there, the exact movements of the children are unknown. They were expected back home on the midday bus, but they never arrived. Nancy Beaumont met the bus, and the children weren't on it. At that point she wasn't overly worried. The children could have decided to walk home, or missed the bus and had to wait for the next one at 2:00pm.

When they weren't on the 2:00pm bus, she began to feel uneasy. She considered going to search for them, but with multiple potential routes to walk home she decided that she could easily miss them, and it was better for her to remain at home in case they came back.

By the 3:00pm bus, the children were still not home. Nancy was now worried enough to call her husband at work and let him know what was going on. He came home and immediately went out searching with Nancy.

By 7:30pm, the parents called the police to officially report the three children missing. Jim Beaumont stayed out searching the entire night.

Investigation:
Between the times the children were last seen at home and when they should have arrived back, at least seven people reported seeing them. Five of the seven reported they saw a man with the children. However, a postman who is thought to be the last to see them said that they were alone.

The man, reported by the five people who saw the children, was observed watching them, and later playing with them under a sprinkler on a grassy area around 11:00am. At 11:45am, the children went to a nearby cake shop and purchased several pastries and a pie using a £1 note. However, the children's parents were insistent that they had only given them eight shillings and sixpence. Had the man perhaps given the children money?

At that point, they were supposed to be on a bus home in fifteen minutes. However, at midday another woman and an elderly couple both saw three children walking past with a man. The man matched the descriptions from the earlier witnesses, and the woman was sure the children were the Beaumonts.

The man approached the witnesses and asked if they had seen anyone interfering with his clothes on the beach, as some money was missing. They said they hadn't seen anything, and he returned to the children. According to the witnesses, the children were friendly with the man, including allowing him to help them put their clothes back on over their swimwear.

Again, their parents later commented how unusual this was, especially for Jane who was a very shy child, and at nine years old, certainly old enough to perform the task for herself. Once dressed, the man picked up a pair of pants and a towel, and he and the children walked away out of sight behind the Glenelg Hotel. By this time it was 12:15pm, and the children had missed their bus home. This was the last time anyone saw either the man or the three children definitively.

At approximately 1:45pm, a man visiting the area from the interstate reported that he saw a man with three children, however the man did not explicitly match earlier descriptions. The postman who saw the children was also unsure whether he had seen the children at the start of his shift in the morning, or later that afternoon. He originally reported that it was in the afternoon, but circumstances led the police to believe it may well have been at the beginning of his shift in the morning instead.

It took until the next morning for the children to be declared missing officially to the public. At the time, it was a comforting fact that children almost never disappear in groups. However, the Beaumont children did not have a reason to run away, and their parents thought that Jane would have stopped any attempt by the younger ones to wander off.

They were therefore left with two options, an accident (most likely drowning) had occurred, or that someone had abducted all three children. From the beginning, the latter looked to be most likely.

Police launched a massive search, reaching miles away from where the children were last seen in all directions. However, no evidence of the children's disappearance, nor any of their belongings were ever found. Even if three children could have been swept out to sea unnoticed on a crowded beach, what happened to their towels, clothes, and other items?

Meanwhile, at their home Nancy Beaumont had to be kept under sedation. Relatives and friends both gathered, waiting for news. The police kept in touch via telephone, and Jim Beaumont also visited the station twice every day.

By the time the weekend arrived, three days later, the missing children were national news, and the search was quickly becoming the biggest ever in Australia. Jim Beaumont used to be a taxi driver, and when word spread, forty cabbies used their cars to join in the search.

The beaches of Adelaide often featured large sand dunes, and they were all meticulously searched, along with every seaside suburb in the area. Police knocked on every single door the children could possibly have passed had they walked home. Hundreds of locals volunteered their own time to search for the three children.

By day five, Jim Beaumont appeared on national television, appealing for their safe return. He broke down, asking for whoever had them to please release them back to their family. Hundreds of leads were phoned in, and while every lead was followed up, nothing ever came of a single one.

The South Australian Police Commissioner even asked people to search their properties, including sheds or abandoned buildings. No one reported finding anything.

By February 3rd, police searched the Patawalonga Boat Haven in Glenelg. Built to give boats easy access to St. Vincent Gulf, police divers searched the deep water while cadets used long forks to search through waist deep mud for the children's bodies. They found nothing.

The same day, Nancy Beaumont first spoke publically, stating that although she was still hopeful, that her children were probably dead. Despite this, the search continued. February passed, and still nothing had been found. By March, an ex-policeman and legendary figure from the New South Wales police force arrived in Adelaide.

Recently retired with the rank of Detective Inspector and likely Australia's most famous policeman, he was employed as a private investigator on the case. However, he left after just one day, not able to find anything new.

Eventually, the search had to be scaled back. Despite the best efforts by the police and hundreds of private citizens, not a single scrap of evidence linking to the children or the mystery man was ever found.

Current Status:

The suspect as described by witnesses was a man in his mid to late thirties, around six feet tall with a thin to athletic build. He had light brown or blonde hair, parted on the left and swept back. Clean-shaven, he had a suntanned complexion and a thin face.

His accent indicated he was from Australia, and he wore blue swimwear with a white stripe down each leg. He also carried a pair of pants and a towel. Four different men were investigated, but no link to the children was ever found.

Police have also followed a number of other leads, but none have revealed any evidence. Sightings continued to be reported for over a year after the children's disappearance. The case even attracted attention from a psychic from the Netherlands. He identified a warehouse nearby where he believed the children were buried.

However, even after demolishing the building due to public pressure, nothing was ever found. Police established that between the three children they were carrying seventeen different items with them. Not a single one has ever been recovered.

Approximately two years after their disappearance, Jim and Nancy Beaumont received a letter apparently written by Jane, along with a man who stated he was keeping the children. It was postmarked in Dandenong, a suburb in Victoria, one state away. Comparing it to Jane's handwriting led police to believe it was quite likely authentic, and the man stated that he was willing to meet up to return the children.

Police attended the designated meet point, but no one ever showed up. Another letter soon arrived, saying that he had been willing to return the children, but then he realized that a detective had been there and so he was keeping them for good.

No other letters ever arrived, and it took another twenty-five years before now improved forensic technology proved that the letters had been a hoax all along.

The disappearance of the Beaumont children is believed to be the trigger for a change of attitude in Australia. No longer was it deemed safe for children to go out without supervision, and they were no longer presumed to be safe on their own. Until then, the freedom given to the children to go out that day was commonplace in Australia.

For many years after their disappearance, Jim and Nancy remained living in the same home in the hope the children would return home looking for them. Eventually, they did sell the home and move away. The case remains open.

A Case That Changed the Law: Johnny Gosch

Missing Person: Johnny Gosch
Date: September 12th, 1982
Last Known Location: Des Moines, Iowa

Backstory:
John David Gosch, known as Johnny, was born on November 12, 1969. He lived in Des Moines, Iowa with his parents, Noreen and John Gosch. He had a part time job as a paperboy.

On The Day In Question:
September 5th, 1982 was a Sunday. Gosch left home before dawn to start his paper route. Usually his father went with him to help, but that day Gosch took only the family dog with him. Other paperboys would later report that they saw Johnny picking up his papers at the paper drop. That was the last time Gosch was definitively seen.

Early that morning, regulars along Gosch's route began to call his parents, complaining their paper had not been delivered. By 6:00am his father, John Gosch was out searching. He found Gosch's wagon, still full with papers, just two blocks from their home. He immediately contacted the police, however Gosch's mother, Noreen Gosch, estimates that it was forty-five minutes before the police arrived at their home.

Investigation:
A neighbor named Mike told police that he had seen Gosch talking to a stocky man, seen driving a two-toned blue Ford Fairlane. The car had Nebraska plates. Mike didn't know what Gosch had spoken about with the man, but he did notice a second man follow Gosch home after he spoke to the man in the car.

Although investigators believed that Gosch had been kidnapped, no evidence was ever found, nor was a motive ever uncovered. Not a single person was ever arrested in conjunction with the investigation.

The investigation uncovered little evidence overall, not even a single suspect was named. Officially, the case remains unsolved. However what happened after that fateful day has left the case of the disappearance of Johnny Gosch under a veil of rumors and speculation for over three decades.

Current Status:

Noreen Gosch remains highly critical of the police response, including the then policy that Gosch could not be officially classified as a missing person until he had been gone for 72 hours. Much of the speculation over the case has come from information Noreen has supplied, information that cannot be substantiated. Is it true, or simply the heartfelt wishes of a grieving mother?

In 1994, a second Des Moines paperboy went missing in similar circumstances. Investigators have never linked the two cases, but Noreen claims she was personally informed of the abduction by a private investigator weeks before it occurred. Almost two years later, a third disappeared in similar circumstances. Neither of those boys has ever been found. The third boy's mother has also been critical of the police, stating that she got the 'distinct feeling' they did not want to be involved in the case.

Noreen Gosch claims that in March 1997, she was woken by a knock on the door around 2:30am. When she opened the door she found her son, now twenty-seven, and another unfamiliar man standing on the doorstep.

She claims she immediately recognized her son, and was able to prove his identity using a birthmark on his chest. They talked for around one and a half hours, and Noreen claims Gosch continually looked to the other man for permission to speak. No one else was present and can corroborate the story.

On September 1, 2006, Noreen again reported an update in the case. This time posting photographs on her website she claimed had been left at her door. The photos show three boys bound and gagged, and she claimed one was Gosch.

The photographs were later deemed by police to be fake, and were taken at an unrelated non-criminal event in Florida. To this day however, Noreen Gosch believes that it is Johnny in the photos.

Some good has come from Gosch's disappearance. In 1984, Noreen Gosch saw a bill she had authored pass into Iowa Law. Named the Johnny Gosch Bill, it mandates that as soon as a child goes missing, police should become involved, rather than waiting the 72 hours.

It has since been adopted by eight other states. She also testified before Congress in 1984, and in part, her testimony led to the establishment of the National Center for Missing and Exploited Children.

A Bright Light Gone Out Too Soon: Jodi Huisentruit

Missing Person: Jodi Huisentruit
Date: June 26th, 1995
Last Known Location: Mason City, Iowa

Backstory:
Jodi Huisentruit was born on June 5th, 1968. She grew up in Long Prairie, Minnesota. Growing up, she had a keen interest in golf, and in her late teens her team won the state's Class A tournament.

Huisentruit went on to study TV Broadcasting and Speech Communication at St. Cloud State University. She graduated in 1990 with a Bachelor's Degree, although her first job after graduation was not in the media, but with Northwest Airlines.

Huisentruit first worked in broadcasting working as the Iowa City bureau chief at KGAN. She then worked at KSAX in Minnesota, before finally returning to Iowa to work for KIMT. At the time of her disappearance, she was working as an anchorwoman for a morning news show.

On The Day In Question:
On June 26th, 1995, Huisentruit joined in on a local golf tournament. According to John Vansice, a resident, she then went to his home where they watched a video of her birthday party that he had organized the previous month. She returned home at approximately 9:00pm, where she called a friend who lived in Mississippi. Her friend reported that Jodi sounded happy and upbeat, with nothing out of the ordinary.

Working as an anchorwoman for a morning news show meant that Huisentruit had an early start on workdays. At 4:00am on June 27th, she hadn't yet arrived at work. Her producer, Amy Kuns, called her at home. Huisentruit answered and said that she'd slept in and was just getting ready to leave. Another call at 5:00am was not answered, and by 6:00am she still had not arrived. A substitute anchor went on camera, and by 7:00am the station staff called the police.

Investigation:
Police first arrived at Huisentruit's apartment and she was gone, but her car (a red Mazda Miata) was still in the parking lot. There was evidence of a struggle near the car, and her personal effects were found lying on the ground, including a pair of shoes, a hairdryer and her keys. The key to the car was bent off in the lock. Police also found forensic evidence on the car, an unidentified handprint. Finally, drag marks were found on the pavement.

Interviews with neighbors found at least three who heard screams around the same time that Huisentruit would have been leaving her apartment to go to work. Another neighbor reported seeing a white van parked near her parking lot, with the parking lights still on. To this day the van has not been seen again or identified.

A team was quickly assembled and they searched the immediate area. When they found nothing, the search was expanded, first to a two-mile radius, then to five and ten, and eventually hundreds of miles from the scene of the crime. To this day, further evidence has not been found. Huisentruit herself has never been found.

Current Status:
As with many cases in this book, rumors quickly spread when the investigation garnered little real evidence. Huisentruit's neighbor, John Vansice, came forward as the last person to see her alive. Huisentruit's brother described Vansice's relationship with her as 'unusual', saying he was fixated on her.

Vansice, twenty years Huisentruit's senior, even named his boat 'Jodi'. A police spokesman has been quoted saying that Vasice remains a person of interest to the case. He believes that Huisentruit knew her attacker. Police found no evidence of a stalker.

Another possibility was a convicted rapist named Tony Jackson, who, at the time of the attack, was living in the same city as Huisentruit. He reportedly refers to a body in rural Jackson County in Iowa in a rap song he wrote in prison. However, an investigation found no link between him and Huisentruit.

Another inmate named Thomas Corascadden also made comments about Huisentruit to officials. However, he passed a polygraph and his palm print did not match the one found at the scene.

In September of the year she disappeared, Huisentruit's family hired a private investigator to try and make a break in the case. With assistance from another P.I. firm in Nebraska, they appeared on national television shows, including America's Most Wanted. In 1997 her family again received attention from the media when they appeared on a television show with well- known psychics.

Both appearances generated many leads, but nothing that ever lead to evidence or a suspect. In the end, police and P.I.'s would together interview more than one thousand people, but find nothing.

In 2011, a woman who worked for the Mason City Police Department for ten years before being fired, came out in public accusing the police department itself of being involved in Huisentruit's disappearance.

She claimed that those high up in the force had actually been responsible, and she had been fired for not handling the information surrounding the case properly. Her accusations were refuted by police.

Jodi Huisentruit was declared legally dead in May of 2001. Her family has never held a funeral. Instead, they host an annual golf tournament in her honor.

Recently, interest in the case has been reignited, due mostly to the creation of a website by local law enforcement and journalists, at findjodi.com. A spokesman says they're optimistic regarding progress and new leads have been coming in.

A Honeymoon Cut Short: George Smith

Missing Person: George Allen Smith IV
Date: June 5th, 2005
Last Known Location: MS Brilliance of the Seas cruise ship, near Turkey

Backstory:
George Allen Smith IV was born on October 3rd, 1978. He lived in Greenwich, Connecticut with his parents George and Maureen Smith and his sister Bree. He ran his family's liquor store, and had just married Jennifer Hagel-Smith. He was twenty-six years old when he disappeared.

On The Day In Question:
Having married his fiancée just eleven days earlier, Smith was on his honeymoon. The newlyweds had taken a cruise in the Mediterranean. The couple had been enjoying the two- week cruise, and Smith had talked about famous people he'd met while on the trip.

On the evening of June 5th, 2005, Smith disappeared from the ship. An investigation found bloodstains near his cabin, and also some on the side of the ship. Crew members suspected that he had either fallen overboard, or that he had been pushed.

Investigation:
From reports, Jennifer Smith awoke the morning after Fourth of July celebrations to find that her husband wasn't in their cabin. She did not immediately raise the alarm, deciding it was likely that he had fallen asleep with new friends they had made, and she went back to sleep herself.

Later, reports would surface that the couple had fought at a disco on board the ship, and that she had later been found passed out in the hallway and returned to her room by the cruise's security guards. This gave her enough of an alibi to remove her as a suspect in her husband's disappearance.

A teenage passenger noticed large red stains on a railing, which could have been bloody fingerprints. Additional red stains found on a lifeboat canopy were cleaned off by staff before they could be investigated.

Investigations revealed that Smith had been drinking that night with a group of young men, including two Russian brothers who now resided in Brooklyn, New York. They were the last to see him alive, and had allegedly taken him back to his room when he became drunk.

On July 29th, 2005, the FBI launched an investigation into Smith's disappearance. They interviewed a man named Josh Askin, who was a student at San Diego State at the time of Smith's disappearance, and was also with him on the night of July 4th.

Michael Jones, the Smith family's lawyer, claims that Askin had failed a polygraph test administered by the FBI when questioned about the events surrounding that night. He claims that Askin also invoked his Fifth Amendment rights when questioned by Mr. Jones.

Jones reported that Askin told his girlfriend that Smith had a large amount of money stored in his cabin, and that Mrs. Smith was playing large hands at the cruise's blackjack tables. Conversely, Askin's lawyer claims that his client passed the polygraph, and only invoked his Fifth Amendment rights when he was told by the FBI he would be prosecuted for perjury if his statements made to them had any discrepancies to his grand jury testimony.

Current Status:
George Smith's family is convinced their son was murdered aboard the cruise ship. His widow received a $1.1 million settlement from the cruise line in 2007. She

has since remarried in 2009. Mrs. Smith is now estranged from the family, and was criticized heavily by them for her behavior on the night their son disappeared. They challenged her settlement with the cruise line.

No further evidence to suggest what truly happened that night on board the ship has ever been found.

Conclusion

There are many cases of persons who have gone missing and never been found. The circumstances, the end results and the locations of the possible remains all continue to be the source of fascination and curiosity for those of us living today.

Certainly we can try to put ourselves in the place of those left to live their lives never knowing what happened, but unless we have experienced it ourselves, we never truly can.

We can only hope that they were able to find some solace and live the rest of their lives in some kind of peace.

Dear Readers,

Thank you for purchasing this book. I enjoyed researching and writing about these cases and I hope you found them to be both interesting and engrossing.

If your friends and family would enjoy reading about this topic, please be sure to let them know about this book.

Again, thank you for your support and I look forward to writing more books of Persons Missing and Lost.

Regards,

Mike Riley

Be sure to check out Mike Riley's other books:

Hollywood Murders and Scandals: Tinsel Town After Dark

"In the late afternoon, her friends recalled, Monroe began to act strangely seeming to be heavily under the influence. She made statements to friend Peter Lawford that he should tell the President goodbye and tell himself goodbye."

Check it out.

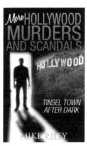

More Hollywood Murders and Scandals: Tinsel Town After Dark

"At some point in the night Reeves and Lemmon began to argue. As Reeves headed upstairs to his bedroom, Lemmon would later tell officers that she shouted out that he would probably shoot himself."

Check it out.

14773980R00043

Printed in Great Britain
by Amazon.co.uk, Ltd.,
Marston Gate.